HABIT:
THE ULTIMATE GUIDE TO BUILDING POWERFUL HABITS THAT STICK ONCE AND FOR ALL

Habits That Stick:

THE Ultimate Guide To Building Powerful Habits That Stick Once And For All

Your Step-By-Step Workbook

YOUR STEP-BY-STEP WORKBOOK

Forming new habits can be difficult, but I've created a step-by-step workbook to help you do just that. Make sure you download it by typing the following URL:
http://whatispersonaldevelopment.org/habits

Thanks,

Thibaut Meurisse

INTRODUCTION

"We are what we repeatedly do. Excellence, then, is not an act, but a habit."-Will Durant

I would like to start by congratulating you for buying this book. Investing your money in a self-improvement book shows me that you're already serious about implementing new habits in your life (and getting rid of old ones that are physically and mentally harmful). It also means that you already have a certain degree of awareness about your current habits and understand that you need to change them in order to live a more fulfilling life.

A LITTLE BIT ABOUT ME

My name is Thibaut Meurisse. I'm originally from France, but I've been living in Japan for the past 8 years. I'm fascinated by personal development and run a blog called What Is Personal Development. During my personal development journey, I became aware of the importance of setting clear goals. Strangely enough, most people don't have clear, written goals that they're working on each day, and even fewer people have goals that fire them up in the morning. That realization is what made me write my first book, which centered on goal-setting. I wanted people to discover that « magical tool ».

I chose to write about habits because I firmly believe that what we do every day is what determines what we'll accomplish in life. Ironically, it was only after many failures that I finally got into the habit of setting goals every day. Turns out goal-setting is its own habit, and, without it, I wouldn't have written the book you're now reading.

It is my sincere hope that this book will help you create solid habits that will serve you for the rest of your life. If you have any questions, feel free to contact me at thibaut.meurisse@gmail.com.

Now, let's get started!

WHAT YOU'LL LEARN IN THIS BOOK:

Within this book, you'll find a comprehensive method to assist you in forming new habits that will support you throughout your life. You won't just learn how to form new habits. You'll also learn how to overcome obstacles and mental blocks to achieve optimal levels of perseverance. This will allow you to keep pushing until you successfully incorporate these new and exciting habits into your daily routine.

This book is inspired by other famous books, so you probably won't find anything fundamentally new in it. You *will, however,* learn the most effective ways to successfully form new habits. You'll be presented with these techniques in a fresh, unique way that is easier to understand and implement. When relevant, I'll also share examples from my own life as well as other insights that I hope will make this book even more valuable to you.

This Book Will Do the Following:

- Provide you with a step-by-step method that will enable you to successfully apply new habits that you'll stick to in the long run.
- Help you unlock your potential and allow you to leverage the power of habit to achieve significantly more in life.
- Support you in getting rid of bad habits
- Assist you in increasing your productivity and happiness by establishing powerful new habits that yield great rewards over time.
- Enable you to avoid or conquer the obstacles that come with creating new habits.
- Give a list of some of the most powerful yet simple habits to have in life.

This book is full of valuable information, but remember, how much you get out of it is largely dependent upon how committed you are to using what you learn. The ball is in your court!

I Want You To Get Results

I really hope that you'll take consistent, massive action and commit yourself to creating powerful, lifelong habits. I believe you bought this book for a specific reason: to form new habits that will change your life and get rid of all the negative habits that prevent you from becoming the person you want to be. Am I right?

Take action and results will follow

I used to be a bookworm, but over the past few years I turned myself into a massive action taker. Why? Because I care about results more so than knowledge. Don't get me wrong, I'm still reading lots of books and loving it, but I always make sure I'm taking as much action as possible each day. Knowledge is certainly power, but knowledge without action is pretty much worthless. On its own, it won't bring you any real results in your life.

I strongly believe that the information in this book is power, but ONLY if you commit to taking action. That's why I went beyond the free step-by-step workbook, I also prepared a 30-Day Challenge to further support you in the process of forming new habits.

Your 30-Day Challenge

This challenge is pretty straightforward. I want you to select one habit (preferably the one that will have the most impact once you've incorporated it into your life) and commit to doing it every day for the next 30 days.

However, there are two traps that I would like to warn you of. First, resist the urge to try forming more than one habit at a time. Focus on ONE habit at a time. Otherwise, the challenge will fail. Secondly, keep in mind that simple doesn't necessarily mean easy. This challenge may seem like a piece of cake to you, but many habits that are easy to do are just as easy NOT to do. A habit is something you do every day, not something you do every other day or whenever the mood strikes you.

WHAT IF YOU COULD PREDICT SUCCESS?

Do you think you can tell whether someone is going to be successful 5 or 10 years from now? You can, believe it or not, and figuring it out is actually very simple. All you have to do is take a look at their typical day. Extraordinary people have extraordinary habits, while average people have average habits. There are very few exceptions to that rule, and it applies to you. So if you want to know where you're going to be in 10 or 20 years from now, look at what you did today or yesterday. As you're reading this book, ask yourself the following question: If I keep doing what I'm doing today, will I be where I want to be in 10 or 20 years from now? Be brutally honest with yourself.

I encourage you to dig deeper by asking this question for each specific goal you have. Look at your goals and ask yourself, "Will I achieve these goals if I keep on doing what I'm doing today?" You'll know the answer if you're honest enough with yourself. How confident are you about your ability to achieve your goals based on what you're currently doing? On a scale of 1 to 10, is your confidence 8 out of 10, 6 out of 10, or even 3 out of 10? If it's less than 8 out of 10, you probably don't have the daily habits that will allow you to successfully achieve your goals. Don't worry, though, this is exactly what we'll be working on in this book. Daily habits aren't necessarily hard to do, but it's VERY easy not to do them at all. That's why you bought this book in the first place, you know you need something to help you stick to your habits.

When asked what keeps you from committing to new habits, you might argue that you were busy today and couldn't do X, Y or Z for whatever reason. You might say that you'll find the time later. The truth is, you can always come up with excuses. But if what you're doing today isn't going to lead you towards a future of fulfillment, happiness and health, there's little reason to believe things will magically change later on.

How often have you heard people say, "I'll start tomorrow"? Whether they're talking about dieting, exercise, or learning a new skill, the result is usually the same. Tomorrow comes and goes but the diet, workout, or activity never starts. And the worst part is, we knew it wasn't going to happen the minute they said "I'll start tomorrow."

NEVER TRUST YOUR FUTURE SELF

If you want to achieve your goals, stick to the following rule: Always assume that what you're doing today is what you'll do tomorrow, next week, next month, next year, and so on and so forth. Doing this focuses your awareness on what you're doing NOW, not what you may (and most likely won't) do in the future. By living as if what you do today will determine your future (it *will*), you'll be motivated to take action in the present instead of relying on your future self to do something later.

Believing that your future self will somehow be more disciplined than your current self is a major trap. Unfortunately, it just doesn't work that way. The fact remains, however, that what your current self does today determines what your future self will do tomorrow!

If what you're doing today isn't going to lead to the future you envision for yourself, it's probably time for you to make some changes in your life. These changes are what we're going to work on together in this book. Now, let's take a deeper look at what habits are.

I. Habits: What They are and Why They're So Hard to Implement

Our lives are largely controlled by our subconscious minds, which are in charge of running the habits we've adopted consciously or, in most cases, unconsciously over the years.

Our brains are very efficient machines that hate wasting energy. Once the brain has been conditioned to perform a certain task repeatedly, it runs primarily on auto-pilot. This is great when you learn to drive or tie your shoes, but it's not so great when you want to break a habit. It takes significant effort to change your brain's preexistent programming, and it's an uphill battle until your subconscious mind finally accepts the change. That's why it's so hard to form new habits or get rid of old ones. Your brain isn't wired for change. It likes things just the way they are.

Why Habits are Mind-Bogglingly Important

The quality of your habits will determine the quality of our life. It's what you do on a daily basis that truly matters, not what you do from time to time or when you have a sudden burst of motivation. Take a few minutes to look at your current habits. How would you describe them? Are they the habits of a successful, happy person? Or are they the habits of someone stuck in a rut?

What a Few Simple Habits Can Do For You

When it comes to habits, it's crucial to realize that even a small daily habit can have a major impact on your life if you stick with them long enough. That's why making habits is powerful yet easy to neglect. **It's no exaggeration to say that you're just a few habits away from success and happiness!** A few good habits can go a long way. On the other hand, a few bad habits like smoking, drinking, or eating unhealthy food can take a major (and even lethal) toll after a while.

The end of this book contains a list of the top 7 daily habits that will bring you the most success in life.

Why Your Success Depends On Your Daily Habits

Your daily habits determine how much you accomplish and are very closely related to your goals. Having consistent daily habits guarantees that you'll be significantly more productive and achieve more in life. Solid daily habits will make it easier to achieve long-term goals. Let's look at some good examples of how daily habits can make a huge difference in the long run:

- Writing 500 words every day will allow you to write a book every 6 months.
- Reading for 30 minutes a day will allow you to finish 200 to 300 books over a 5-year period.
- Meditating for 15 minutes every day will enhance your long-term happiness.
- Spending 5 minutes a day on gratitude exercises will also increase your overall happiness.

Why You Are Wasting Your WillPower Without Knowing It!

Unfortunately willpower is a limited resource. You can either use all of your willpower and brute force your way into getting your tasks done each day, or you can invest it strategically to create new, powerful habits that will serve you for years to come. Think of habits as a return on the investment of your willpower. More specifically, **habits are returns on the investment of willpower that has been strategically directed towards their formation**.   Some use their precious willpower wisely and put it towards creating one or two positive new habits, while others waste it in an attempt to create too many habits at once. Still others do absolutely nothing with their willpower, which wastes tremendous opportunities for growth. It's all up to you, but I strongly recommend the first option!

THE INCREDIBLE POWER OF FOCUSED WILLPOWER

Putting your willpower towards the creation of habits will enable you to automatize many of your tasks and turn you into a well-oiled machine. Once a habit is accepted by your subconscious mind, you will need little to no willpower to maintain it every day. Think about when you first learned to drive a car, for example. Do you remember how overwhelming it was? There were so many things going on at once, all of which required your full attention. Now, however, it's become automatic, and the entire process is taken care of by your subconscious mind. In fact, there may be times when you barely remember driving to and from home, work, and other familiar places.

That's the power of the subconscious mind, and this process holds true for habits. If you apply focused willpower to a specific task every day, it's only a matter of time before it becomes automatic.

Do you think highly successful people are virtuosos or geniuses? While this is occasionally true, most people are successful simply because they developed powerful daily habits that allowed them to become extremely efficient. The good news is that you, too, can develop these habits.

If you can learn to use your willpower to form new, powerful, daily habits that will stay with you long-term, you're in for a treat. You'll experience heightened efficiency and effectiveness, in addition to significantly increasing your levels of happiness and fulfillment.

There's a lot at stake, so make sure you invest your willpower wisely each and every day.

WHAT A TRULY OUTSTANDING HABIT REALLY LOOKS LIKE

When you implement new habits, you want to make sure they'll have a legitimate impact on your life in the long run. Otherwise, why bother? It may be hard to figure out how much of an impact certain habits will have on your life, but it's much easier when you know what a good habit looks like. Good habits should:

- Be something you want to maintain for the rest of your life.
- Significantly impact your productivity, happiness, fulfillment, or anything else that you genuinely value.
- Support you in achieving your long-term goals.
- Be within your sweet spot. You should feel confident that you can stick to them in the long run, even when the going gets rough.
- Have a strong "why" behind them (i.e. there should be a compelling reason as to why are they're so important to you).
- Be performed at a specific time during the day or have a clear *trigger.

*See the trigger section of this book for more details.

If you haven't yet make sure you download your free workbook by typing the following URL in your browser: www.whatispersonaldevelopment.org/habit

II. Bad Habits: What They Are and How to Get Rid of Them

The habits that have the most impact on your life are often a reflection of who you *think* you are. If you do something for long enough, it becomes closely related to your identity.

For instance, many people who smoke cigarettes associate this habit with who they are as a person. They don't see themselves as a person who happens to have one (or many) cigarettes each day. Rather, they see themselves as a label, and refer to themselves as a smoker. Many people who struggle with their weight fail to see themselves as a person who is carrying extra weight. They simply think of themselves as overweight. People often think of themselves as the adjectives that describe the side effects of their habits or the habit itself (think labels like 'smoker' or 'overeater').

You may be wondering how much this matters. It actually matters a lot, because it's hard to change something that is part of the way you define yourself. So, what do you do if you realize you've been defining yourself by your habits, or the results of your habits?

The first step, as silly as it may sound, is to start questioning your identity very seriously. After all, there was a time in your life when you didn't identify with these things at all, right? There was a time when you didn't even know what a cigarette tasted like, and there was probably a time in your life, however early, where you were at a weight that was healthy for you. *You* are not a smoker. You are simply someone who smokes. *You* are not fat. You are simply someone whose habits have resulted in some extra weight.

It all comes down to habits, and just as your habits caused you to smoke or gain weight, habits can cause you to stop smoking and achieve the weight that is healthiest for your body. The *real* you can't be changed that easily.

In a way, these identities are just ideas in your mind. Repetition brought them into your reality and eventually made them part (or even all) of your identity. Fortunately, it doesn't have to stay that way.

If you want to change habits that have become part of your identity, you need to figure out who you are and who you want to be. Are you the type of person who walks every day and takes the stairs instead of the escalator? Are you the type of person who doesn't smoke in the morning? Are you someone who eats sweets in moderation?

So start questioning your identity every day. Are you really the label that you've placed on yourself? What does it really mean?

WHAT YOUR BAD HABITS SAY ABOUT YOU

We all have bad habits that we're trying to get rid of. Nobody is perfect and the point is not to get rid of *all* your bad habits. That's a sure way to set yourself up for failure and crush your self-esteem. When certain habits prevent you from being happy and healthy, however, it's time to change them.

The Emotions Behind Your Bad Habits

Believe it or not, all habits serve some kind of purpose. Even your worst habits provide you with some kind of emotional benefit. If they didn't you wouldn't have them, or you could drop them with ease. It's very difficult to get rid of bad habits if you don't know why you have them in the first place. There may be a habit that helps you procrastinate and avoid things that you're afraid of, for instance, or one that helps you cope with stress. Most, if not all, of your bad habits are disguised attempts to escape from something in your life.

HOW TO GET RID OF BAD HABITS

Keep in mind that certain types of habits, such as those that have turned into physical addictions like alcoholism, are beyond the scope of this book. Addictions are another matter entirely. That said, I'd like to touch upon the subject of breaking habits and explain what you can do to get rid of *most* of your bad habits.

You must start by becoming more aware of the reasons behind your habits. You need to clearly identify what emotional needs they're meeting in your life.

BE MINDFUL OF YOUR HABITS – THE POWER OF AWARENESS

I believe self-awareness is one of the most powerful ways to get rid of bad habits forever and implement new, positive ones. The fact that you bought this book proves that, to a certain extent, you're already aware of some of your habits and how they might be dragging you down.

Take some time to look at the bad habits you'd like to change. Select just one for now. Are you aware of the emotions associated with that habit? Do you see why you have this habit and why it's so hard to get rid of? Does this habit help you cope with your fears? Is it a means of escaping from something? If so, from what?

BELIEVE THAT YOU CAN

It may sound like common sense, but you have to believe that you can actually get rid of this habit. So let me ask you: do you believe you can do it? Can you honestly answer yes to that question?

Most of what happens to us in life is the result of our beliefs. Beliefs are incredible, they can be your best friend or your worst enemy. The answer to the previous question is: Yes. Yes, you can! You are more than capable of eliminating your bad habit. However bad your habit may be, there are people out there just like you who've gotten rid of the same habit.   Their ability to do this was rooted in two things: believing that they could get rid of their unwanted habit, and fully committing to doing so.

100% COMMITMENT

Are you COMPLETELY committed to changing your habit? Really? When it comes to changing a bad habit, you have to commit to it with every fiber of your being. Does this sound obvious, too? Getting rid of a bad habit is far from easy. Chances are, you've tried unsuccessfully in the past, and you may fail again in the future. The question is: can you commit to getting rid of that bad habit despite the obstacles you may face? Can you stick to it no matter how long it takes? Can you get back up when you fail? When the going gets tough, will you stay committed to eliminating the pesky habit that's preventing you from being the person you want to be?

Can you honestly say that you'll get rid of your habit no matter what?

TAKE FULL RESPONSIBILITY

You can't be fully committed to getting rid of your bad habit unless you take responsibility for the situation you're in now. When you don't take complete responsibility for your life, you give your power away to circumstances, situations, and people. By refusing to acknowledge that you have the power to change your current situation, you give up all hope of eliminating your bad habit.

You may be drinking because you have a problem at home or at work. You may gamble excessively or play video games all day because you want to escape your day-to-day reality. Regardless of the pressures fueling these bad habits, they still come from choices you have made. As such, the commitment and decision to stop must also come from you.

Are you currently taking responsibility for your bad habit, or are you blaming other people and things for it? If you think you're drinking because your job is stressful or things aren't going well in your relationship, you are wrong. You are the one who chooses to use alcohol to escape. It all comes down to how YOU choose to deal with the situation. Nobody is forcing you to do anything. It may be a bitter pill to swallow, but it's the truth. If you play the victim, you'll be stuck forever. Take responsibility for your life because, situations, circumstances, and people rarely change. If you want change, it has to come from within.

How to Get Rid of Most Bad Habits

Let's look at some examples of what I call "mild addictions". This term covers the kind of bad habits addressed in this book.

Let's say you're spending 3 hours a day playing video games and you'd like to get rid of that habit. Figure out what emotional needs the games are filling? Are you using them as a way to escape your responsibilities? Do they help you deal with stress at work or in your personal life?

You could be using your bad habit as a way to procrastinate, or it could be a mild addiction related to the instant gratification that you receive from it. Television, social media, video games, and food are prime examples of these types of habits. In fact, they are largely designed to hook you in by exploiting a "biological loophole" that advertising takes full advantage of. You've probably   noticed how each episode of your favorite shows ends in a way that makes you obsessed with seeing the next one. And if you're like most people, you've probably found yourself binging on television shows.

When you step back and look at the big picture, however, you'll see that video games, television shows, and social media platforms that look so appealing on first glance don't really contribute to your happiness and well-being.

We're wired to respond to instant gratification in whatever form it comes. Even so, with enough commitment, awareness, and preparation, we can eradicate our bad habits. I'll explain this more in upcoming sections.

OBSERVE YOUR EMOTIONS WITHOUT BEING JUDGMENTAL

What emotions do you feel before, during, and after you engage in your bad habit? Do you feel excitement right before it starts? What about during it? Is the excitement still there after it's over, or do you experience feelings of guilt or dissatisfaction? It's important that you take the time to observe your emotions during each phase without judging them. Now, let's take an in-depth, step-by-step look at these 3 phases. For simplicity's sake, let's use video games as our example.

Before

How do you feel when you get the urge to play video games? Stay with that feeling, observe it with the kind of curiosity and objectivity you would expect from a scientist. Stop yourself from acting on it just for a while. Don't try to ignore it or turn it down. Then, try to recall how you felt the last time you finished playing video games (see "After" section below). Did you feel happier, more fulfilled, or more confident?

At this point, you should tell yourself that you'll play video games in 5 minutes, but just want to do something else that you enjoy first. This could be reading a book, listening to your favorite song, or playing an instrument. It really doesn't matter what it is as long as you like the activity. The higher your chances of becoming absorbed in it, the better.

How This Helps:

- Becoming more conscious of the feelings you have when you're about to dive into your bad habit allows you to start gaining control over the situation.
- Delaying the moment you'll start engaging in your habits helps you   condition to stop acting on impulse.
- Starting a different activity for a few minutes shifts your focus away from your habit, especially if the other activity is something you particularly enjoy. You can then delay the moment you start your bad habit even further whenever possible. You may even skip it altogether sometimes! As you repeat this process, you'll become better and better at resisting the urge to act on your emotions.

During

Observe the emotions you feel while playing video games with the same curiosity and objectivity that we discussed above. How do you feel? Are you really enjoying the process? Or is it less pleasurable than you thought it would be?

Create multiple interruptions as you're playing by taking breaks or doing something else for just a few moments. Stop to get a drink, go to the bathroom, or tidy up your area. These interruptions can come at intervals of your choosing. You could set a timer to stop playing once every twenty minutes, or you might decide to take a break whenever your feelings about playing fluctuate. Make sure these interruptions are given a genuine effort, though. Pause the game, turn off the television, or whatever action applies, take a moment to become conscious of how you feel, then start your other activity. Try sitting or standing somewhere else, or go to another room if possible.

During this process, it's important to give yourself total permission to go back playing video games at any time. Don't blame yourself, don't try to force yourself to resist the urge to return to them. Go back to playing video games if you feel like it, or keep on with your other activity. Either one is fine.

Why it Works:

- Staying in touch with your emotions heightens your self-awareness, which leaves room for alternatives to your habit, such as taking a break or doing something else. This will make it much easier to cut back on or totally eliminate your habit, depending on which option is healthiest (remember, some things are fine in moderation).
- By turning off the TV, pausing the game, or taking a break, you interrupt the "trance", at which point you may realize that playing video games wasn't as fulfilling as you expected. As you start other activities, you may become so absorbed with them that you forget the urge to engage in your bad habit.
- Have you ever forgotten to do something you really wanted to do because you were interrupted or started doing something else? I've done this on a number of occasions, and that's exactly what we're recreating here. When you're caught up in a certain activity, it often seems as if you just can't stop. As soon as you get distracted and start doing something else, however, you break

the spell and often wonder why you were so absorbed in the previous activity.

After

Pay close attention to how you feel after you're done playing video games. Are you satisfied and happy? Or does it feel as if you wasted your time again just like yesterday and the day before it? Do you experience guilt? Stay with your feelings, whatever they may be. Then, imagine what else you could have done instead of playing video games?

Keep a time log where you write exactly how much time you engage in your bad habit. Do this for at a week, then multiply the results by 52 to figure out how much time it takes out of your year. How many hours do you spend playing video games, watching TV, gambling, etc. What else could you have done with all that time?

If your habit is something you do multiple times a day, like checking emails or going on Facebook, use an app that will record how much time you spend doing that. You can also keep a piece of paper by your computer and use it to record every time you check social media or emails. These tactics might sound simple, but they'll force you to become more conscious of your actions   and take note of what you're actually doing. You might be shocked by how many times you check your emails or social media accounts each day!

Why it Works:

- By getting in touch with the shame, guilt, frustration, and negative feelings that come after you've engaged in your habit, you'll begin to associate the activity with pain. You'll realize that, in retrospect, it never feels as good as you think it will. Remember those painful emotions each time you're tempted. Are you sure you want to feel that again?
- Keeping a time log forces you to become more conscious of your activities and sheds light on how much time you're really

spending on that not-so-fulfilling habit. It compels you to face a harsh but necessary reality.

REPLACE BAD HABITS WITH BETTER ONES

Eliminating unsavory habits is only part of the process. It's important to understand that replacing negative habits with better and more positive ones is much more effective than simply trying to get rid of bad habits.

If you decide to stop playing video games three hours every day, what are you going to do instead? If you have no clear plan on how to use that time, you'll very likely go back to your old habits. Your brain likes the status quo, so, if you don't give it anything else to focus on, it will guide you back to playing video games.

In the previous section, I mentioned interrupting your activity to do something else you enjoy. So what was this other activity that you enjoy? Surely there's more than one. What kind of things could you do that can get wrapped up in pretty quickly? Maybe it's reading and writing? Or perhaps it's cooking? What about exercising? Chances are, you have plenty of options. Just ask yourself the following question: What activity could satisfy the emotional needs that I've been using my bad habit to cope with?

Additional Tip: Consider recording your emotions before, during, and after your bad habit for 7 days straight. This will ensure that you're doubly aware of your emotions and will increase your mindfulness.

VISUALIZE THE FUTURE COST OF TODAY'S BAD HABITS

Can you imagine what your life will be like 20 years from now if you fail to eliminate that bad habit? When it comes to improving our lives, imagination is one of the most powerful tools we have. Our imaginations allow us to use our minds to create whatever experiences we want at any given time. You can enjoy various scenarios and situations in your mind as often as you like without spending a dime. This is why professional athletes, chess players, army generals, CEOs, and other successful people use visualization on a daily basis.

We all use visualization, even if it's on a subconscious level. The problem is that, if you're like most people, you're probably visualizing negative things. You might be worrying about the future and visualize yourself losing your job or failing an exam. You might also be dwelling on and visualizing the past.

In the exercise below, we're going to use both positive and negative visualization to help you get rid of your bad habits. I learned this exercise from Leo Gura's Youtube video "Bad Habits – A Live Exercise For Dropping Any Bad Habits For Good". You can check out his video to help you through the exercise. But now, for a brief explanation of how it works:

Visualize Your Negative Habit

- Visualize yourself engaging in your bad habit throughout the day. How does it make you feel?
- Now visualize yourself doing it for the next 30 days.
- Next, imagine yourself doing it for a whole year. Imagine the disappointment of the people around you, and think of how it will negatively impact your life.
- Finally, imagine yourself 10 years from now. Visualize the habit getting stronger, as habits almost always grow stronger with time. How do you feel? Focus on the pain associated with having had this destructive habit in your life for a decade. How has it impacted your life? How would that prevent you from reaching your potential and living a truly fulfilling life?

Visualize Your Positive Habit

- Visualize your new positive habit, and imagine yourself doing it today. What feelings does this bring up?
- Now, visualize yourself sticking to this new habit for the next 30 days.

- Next, imagine engaging in this habit for an entire year. How does it affect your life? How much difference does it make? Imagine its benefits, and what it has allowed you to accomplish.
- Finally, imagine yourself 10 years down the line with the new habit still in place. How has this new habit transformed your life? What impact has it had on those around you? How much happiness and fulfillment has it brought you?

Visualization is a very powerful tool, but it becomes increasingly effective when it's done repeatedly over long periods of time. You should try to use visualization as often as possible. If visualization is something that resonates with you, I encourage you to take a few minutes every day to go through this exercise.

The next portion of this book includes concepts from a section of my productivity book that can be applied to the making and breaking of habits. Understanding these concepts will help you find the motivation to work on the activity that will replace the habit you're trying to eliminate. Procrastination is the primary concept covered in this section, and it's the enemy of creating positive habits. Think about it. If you put off the activities that are supposed to replace your bad habits, what's going to happen? You guessed it! You'll go right back to your old habit. Bad habits die hard!

FROM PROCRASTINATION TO ACTION

"Procrastination is the bad habit of putting off until the day after tomorrow what should have been done the day before yesterday." - *Napoleon Hill*

As I've said before, the urge to procrastinate is often strongest just as we begin to work on our most important tasks. Procrastination is a huge obstacle that can seriously limit your productivity. On one hand, you're driven by fear and a powerful urge to escape. On the other, you're really passionate about what you're trying to do and want to start working on it already.

The question is: how do you replace the paralysis of procrastination with action?

It's not going to be easy, but the following three-step formula will help tremendously:

1. Eliminate Distractions

The first order of business is to leave as little room for distractions as possible. When you feel the urge to procrastinate, you'll find yourself interested in anything but your task. Stay one step ahead of distractions by identifying potential **procrastination patterns**. When are you wasting time and why? Is it procrastination or inefficient prioritizing that's draining your time?

Use the results of your time log investigation to create a **Not-To-Do List** based on the results you get from the time log and put the list on your desk. My list looks something like this:

-Don't check emails

-Don't check Facebook or other social media

-Don't go on YouTube or Google

-Don't go for a walk

-Don't check my phone

-Don't eat

-Don't check my book sales on Amazon

-Don't go to the convenience store to buy a drink

The next line of defense is removing all distractions from your desk. You should also plan your tasks in advance, prepare your environment, and give yourself a way to jot down intrusive thoughts. Keep phones, books, food, and other such items far away. The day before you start working on your task, spend some time visualizing yourself doing it.

This will help you condition your mind and decrease the risk of distractions.

You can prepare your environment by readying the tools you'll need for your task ahead of time. Make sure everything is easily accessible. Do any and everything you can to make things as effortless as possible.

Last but not least, keep a piece of paper on hand in case something pops into your mind as you're working. Use it to write down any ideas or lightbulb moments that come to you. Otherwise, you'll remember something you forgot to do and decide to work on it... only to end up spending an hour on Facebook.

2. Become Aware of Your Fears and Emotions

Get in touch with the feelings that come up as you gear up to work on your task.

- Be aware of your feelings when you start working on an important task
- Use a time log to bring awareness on the way you're using your time

3. Reduce the Friction Associated with Starting the Task

It's essential to reduce the discomfort involved in beginning your task. You can accomplish this through visualization. Consider your current feelings and imagine how you'll feel once your task is completed. If that doesn't work, just start and see what happens. Tell yourself you'll only work for a few minutes. You can handle almost anything for five minutes, right?

If fear is still getting the best of you, accept the possibility that you may not do as good of a job as you'd like. Make it okay to do poorly. The reality is that you probably won't do badly unless you're extremely tired. And if you *really* think you'll do a subpar job, what makes you think you'll do any better tomorrow or next week? After all, your plan was to work on it *today*.

III. How to Implement Rock-Solid Habits That Really Stick

Now that we've covered bad habits, let's move on to the exciting part: How to implement new, positive habits that will bring great results and more fulfillment in life.

Are you ready?

Failing To Plan Is Planning To Fail

In this section we're going to talk about the importance of preparation when you implement a new habit into your life.

Mental Preparation: Getting Your Mind on Board

The most common reason we fail when attempting to build new habits or work on new goals is lack of mental preparation. If you bought this book, chances are you've tried and failed to form new habits many times in the past. Before you give it another (and might I add successful) try, you have to ask yourself exactly why your previous attempts failed. Was it because you tried to implement too many habits at once? Did you lack a strong, intrinsic motivation to break the habit? Were you trying to do it for someone else rather than yourself? Or was it hard to fully believe in yourself? These are common sources of failure, but the reason behind yours might be completely different. Take some time to refer to the workbook and reflect upon the reasons your previous attempts have failed.

Anticipate Obstacles

Now that you're clearly aware of the reasons behind your previous failures, it's time to prepare yourself mentally. To do that, you must anticipate the obstacles that may prevent you from forming your new habit and sticking to it in the long run. After all, what's the point of implementing a new habit if you drop it after a few months? Before starting your new habit, you have to take into account all the mental blocks you may have. Consider the following questions: How confident are you that you can stick to this new habit? What are some potential obstacles that could lead you to give up?

Believing in Yourself

Do you believe you can stick to your new habit? If I were to ask you on a scale of 1 to 10 how confident are you that you'll be able to stick to it for the next 30 days what would you say? If your score isn't 8 or more you might need to chunk down your habit to make it more realistic and more believable.

Now that you know where you stand regarding your new habit, can you identify all the possible reasons why you could fail?

Prepare Yourself for Obstacles

Things rarely go as planned and there are many things that may stand in your way as you try to establish new habits in your life. It's essential to take the time to identify the roadblocks you may face with as much clarity as possible. So, what challenges do you think you're likely to encounter?

Let me give you an example of what your list may look like. Let's assume your goal is to stick to your new diet, which includes reducing your sugar intake. Let's further assume you've decided to do this by breaking your habit of drinking sodas and choosing low-sugar beverages instead.

In this case, you might face the following obstacles:

- Dinner with friends, because it's difficult to eat healthy when everyone around you is eating tempting foods and drinking the sodas you are trying so hard to avoid.
- Fast-food chains, because you can easily grab unhealthy food and drinks on your way to work.
- Emotional eating, because people tend to crave sugar when stressed.
- Lack of support. If you're the only one in your family or circle of friends who's watching what they eat, it's going to be difficult. It

isn't easy sticking to your habits while watching others indulge in the very things you're trying to avoid.

- A weak "why" because you know you *should* eat healthy but don't feel motivated enough to do so.

When considering these obstacles, it's a good idea to figure out what triggers you to drink soda and what you can do to work around it. You might purge your fridge of all unhealthy beverages, join a support group, or enlist your friends to help you stay on track when you're going out with them. If you've made a past attempt at a similar diet that didn't go well, you should think about why it didn't work out and see what you can learn from that experience. It's also advisable to sort through your underlying thoughts surrounding food. Perhaps you associate certain foods or even excessive eating and drinking with enjoyable activities such as going to the movies, hanging out with friends, or spending time with family. Or maybe you associate them with comfort and use them to cope with unpleasant feelings and situations. If any of these things is the case, it would be wise to adopt new beliefs that don't support these unhealthy associations and links.

Now it's your turn. What are some obstacles you're likely to encounter and how will you overcome them? How will you address each of these obstacles, and what can you do to minimize them? Take some time now to write down your answers using the downloadable worksheet.

HAVE A PREEMPTIVE PLAN

"Optimism can make us motivated, but a dash of pessimism can help us succeed. Research shows that predicting how and when you might be tempted to break your vow increases the chances that you will keep a resolution."- Kelly McGonigal, The Willpower Instinct.

Now I'd like to imagine yourself in some of the scenarios you wrote down in your list of obstacles. What will you do when one of these situations arises?

By preparing yourself mentally and rehearsing how you'll deal with challenging situations in the future, you'll significantly increase your ability to resist temptation and stay on track with your goals.

In the instance of the low-sugar diet, you could visualize yourself entering a Starbucks and ordering a coffee with no sugar or another drink with a minimal amount of sugar. This may not be enough to prevent temptation entirely.   It will, however, make it easier to make the right choice instead of acting on impulse. You could also visualize yourself opening the fridge and taking a bottle of water instead of a soda. As you continue to visualize yourself making healthy decisions, you'll increase your chances of successfully dealing with real-life temptation.

The "If... Then" Method

This is a highly effective approach to minimizing your chances of reverting to your old habits. In a nutshell, this method involves creating alternatives to what you're trying to avoid. This drastically decreases the risk of making the wrong choice.

Example:

- **If** I'm out with my friends, everybody is drinking soda, and I feel a strong urge to order one, too, **then** I will order a coke zero instead.
- **If** I see a Starbucks, **then** I will cross the street.

Okay, now it's time for you to give it a go. Based on your previous list, how can you use the If...Then Method to create powerful alternatives to your bad habit?

YOU ARE THE PRODUCT OF YOUR ENVIRONMENT

We've already discussed how you can use visualization to mentally prepare yourself for coping with tempting scenarios. In this section, however, we'll go one step further by discussing how you can change your physical environment to reduce or even eliminate the obstacles on your list.

Let me start by sharing a short anecdote from my own life. I first noticed how powerful our environment is while eating nuts that I kept on my desk. I didn't even realize I was eating them until a brief moment of clarity interrupted my then-typical lack of awareness . When I discovered that I was eating nuts without even thinking about it, it made me wonder what else I might be doing unconsciously. It hit me that I would have eaten whatever was on my desk, be it chips, cookies, or carrots, without even noticing.

This simple story illustrates how much we are influenced by our environment. As someone with a sweet tooth, I would sometimes "binge" on cake and other sweets. Once I became aware of this tendency, I stopped buying sweets. If you were to come to my apartment, you'd be hard-pressed to find candy or pastries.   When I happen to receive a food-related package from my parents for Christmas, it generally results in some unhealthy "binge eating". I'll be the first to admit that this may indicate a lack of discipline on my part. But, it also shows that, when it comes to habits, minimizing temptations within your environment can go a long way.

Making strategic changes to your environment will allow you to limit the amount of willpower you expend when performing your daily habit. You don't want to leave any room for excuses and distractions, nor do you want to create unnecessarily tempting situations when you're just getting started. If, for instance, you want to replace unhealthy foods and drinks with nutritious meals and water, the last thing you want is a fridge full of chocolate milk and frozen pizzas. Having chocolate milk in plain sight might not be good idea either.

Here are a few more examples of some of the ways that you can make your environment more conducive to developing new habits:

Example 1: Keeping your home free of junk food and your workspace clear of unhealthy snacks to avoid compulsive eating. I've mentioned this before, but it bears repeating.

Example 2: Keeping your running shoes by your bed if you're trying to make a habit of going for morning runs when you wake up.

Example 3: Putting cigarettes in a place that's difficult to access if you're trying to stop smoking. Or, storing them at a friend or relative's place so that you have to ask them each time you want to smoke.

SURROUNDING YOURSELF WITH THE RIGHT PEOPLE

Another major component of engineering a favorable environment is surrounding yourself with the right people. I once read a quote which stated the following: *If you want to lose weight you should surround yourself with skinny people.* Strange as it may sound, I've found the concept behind this quote to be very true.

I'm a firm believer of the power of surrounding yourself with people that have the kind of life you want. If your friends are all health-conscious, it's obvious that there will be fewer temptations to eat unhealthy food when you go out with them. I'm not saying you should get rid of all your friends (though in certain cases it may be necessary). What I am saying is that you should surround yourself with as many people who encourage and exemplify your goals as possible.

Now that you've mentally prepared yourself and altered your environment to support your new habit, let's look at how you can strengthen your commitment and make this new habit stick.

HOW MUCH SKIN DO YOU HAVE IN THE GAME?

GIVE IT 100%

How often have you started something half-heartedly and wound up not getting results? The best example of this is those famous (or is it infamous?) New Year's resolutions. To be frank, I think New Year's resolutions are pretty ridiculous. I can't help but wonder why I should wait until the beginning of next year to start setting some goals and improve my life.   But I digress. The main problem with New Year's resolutions is that most people who set them fail. The reason behind this is simple: People who rely on New Year's resolutions to make changes don't have clear goals. If they had monthly and yearly goals, they wouldn't need New Year's resolutions. Because they don't have a good understanding of how goal-setting actually works, their resolutions end in failure. Sadly, this isn't surprising, considering what a powerful yet underused tool goal-setting is. It's so underused, in fact, that I actually wrote an entire book on it to help my readers master it.

Now, coming back to commitment, let's be honest. You can't really achieve anything if you aren't 100% devoted to it. In this section, I'll discuss some important points you need to consider when working on your new habit.

Understanding Your Why

It's difficult to be fully devoted to achieving something when you don't have a strong reason behind it. Think about some of the habits that you've tried to continually implement in the past only to fail miserably each time. We all have them. If you hate cleaning, for instance, it's going to be difficult to turn cleaning your house into a daily habit. You may understand from a logical standpoint that you should clean your place, but if you're honest with yourself, you don't really care (wait, am I talking about myself here?). My lack of excitement for cleaning aside, if a particular habit isn't all that important to you, you won't see clear benefits to it. And that is precisely why you'll fail. To avoid this, you would have to give cleaning a new meaning. Otherwise, it's not going to happen.

Should vs. Want

Now, back to the new habit you'd like to implement. What words do you use when you talk about it? If you say something along the lines of "I should do X" then there's a good chance that this is a habit you think you should adopt due to external pressure. This pressure can come from a variety of sources, such as your parents, friends, and colleagues, or even society itself. If, however, you tend to say "I *want* to do X", it's likely that it's something that means a lot to you personally. As such, it will be easier for you to rely on intrinsic motivation, which increases your chance of success.

What if My "Why" Isn't Strong?

If you discover you don't have a particularly strong "why" behind your habit, don't panic. There are ways to work around this.   Going back to our previous example of wanting to tidy up on a daily basis while battling a hatred of cleaning, let's take a look at what you can do when your "why" is weak.

Solution 1: Use reframing to change what the task means to you.

If you don't associate cleaning with anything positive, you could train yourself to see it from a different, more positive point of view. For example, would you clean your house if you had guests coming tonight? If the answer is yes, that tells me you care what others think about the way your home looks. It also tells me that neglecting to clean your place in that circumstance would cause feelings of shame and potentially lower your self-esteem. That means cleaning your home could be seen as part of taking care of yourself and bolstering your self-esteem. You obviously care enough about your guests to do some cleaning. Why would you do something for them that you're not willing to do for yourself? Doesn't that seem like a sign of low self-esteem? You should care enough about tidying up on a regular basis and, when you think of it this way, cleaning probably sounds a lot more appealing. The great thing is that this type of reframing can be applied to any other habit that lacks a strong "why".

Solution 2: Delegate the task.

As simple as it may sound, you could decide to delegate or outsource the task. If no amount of reframing can change the fact that you hate cleaning and see little value in it, it's probably not a wise way to use your time. Why not spend a little bit of money and hire someone to clean every once in a while? You can then invest the time you would have spent cleaning into more meaningful tasks.

WRITE DOWN YOUR HABIT

Writing down your habits and goals is the first step to turning them into reality. I like to write both daily and long-term goals on paper. In my goal-setting book I mention in more details the benefits of writing your goals down, and how to do so effectively. For right now, however, let's focus on how to go about recording your habits.

At this point, you should have already written down the new habit you want to add to your life. If you haven't, grab a pen and paper or use the workbook to write down exactly what your new habit is. Then, write down what makes it important to you.

Ideally, you should read the "what" and "why" of your habit out loud every day to strengthen and maintain your commitment.

HAVE AN ACCOUNTABILITY PARTNER

Another powerful way to stick to your new habit is to have an accountability partner. Having an accountability partner that can monitor your progress, provide motivation, and give advice is tremendously helpful. Some people even hire life coaches for this very reason, they want someone to support them as they make positive life changes. An accountability partner can be anyone that motivates, encourages, and supports you. Feel free to consider me as your accountability partner as you go through your 30-Day-Challenge. It would be quite an honor for me.

Being held accountable by another person has another benefit: It provides a major incentive to follow through. You don't want to have to tell someone that you didn't do what you promised you would, or that you fell off the wagon. And you certainly don't want to disappoint someone who believes in and is rooting for you.

You may want to take this benefit a step further by incorporating consequences. It could be something as simple as agreeing to give a certain amount of money to your accountability partner if you fail to stick to your habit.

Something like that is great because it forces you to ask yourself an indirect but extremely important question: How much do I believe in my ability to stick to my habit? If you're scared of betting money, then you don't fully believe in yourself. Being willing to bet money shows that you're completely committed and really believe in yourself. The more you're willing to bet, the truer this is.

So take a few moments to think about your levels of commitment and self-belief. How much money are you willing to bet that you'll stick with your new habit for the next 30 days. $10? $100? $1,000?

To further illustrate the power of commitment, let me give you a simple example from my daily life that happened to me. My dentist recently told me to start a regimen of daily exercises to correct a jaw issue. I didn't feel I had the time for the exercises and I couldn't find the motivation to do them. But I still promised her that I would do the exercises every day for a month. I even specified the time of day that I would do them. So, do you think I'm doing my exercise now? You bet I am! After all, my dentist will be able to tell whether I've done the exercises when I go to my next appointment, and I don't want to be put on the spot and forced to admit that I failed to do what I said I would. Despite my lack of enthusiasm for them, the exercises are now part of my morning ritual. This example might sound silly, but it speaks volumes about the power of accountability.

Is there anyone you have in mind for your accountability partner? It may take some time to find someone who fits the bill, but it will ultimately happen. So, let's discuss what you should do once you find the right person.

When you talk to your accountability partner, you should discuss the following:

Your habit

Talk about what your habit is (in as much detail as possible) and how the two of you will know if you've succeeded in implementing it. Decide how many days you'll commit to. Will you stick to your habit for 30 days? 60? Perhaps 90? Pin down the length of time and set a date.

What You're Committing To

Come up with a clear declaration of exactly what you intend to do. If, for instance, you want to start working out on a daily basis, you would say "I'm making a commitment to go to the gym every morning for the next 30 days."

Why This Habit Matters to You

Go over what you'll gain from honoring your commitment, and contemplate the consequences of failing to establish the habit.

What You Expect From One Another

This subject should be covered in great detail. Establish their wants and needs as well as your own. And, most importantly, make sure you're both on the same page regarding your partnership.

How You'll Relay Your Progress

Decide how you'll keep in touch. Some people prefer emails or text messages, others prefer phone calls, and still others prefer face-to-face communication. Pick the method of communication that's best for you both. Last but not least, determine how often you'll update them on your progress.

Consequences

Figure out what will happen if you succeed or fail. Will there be rewards for your success, and if so, what will they be? What about penalties? Reneging on your commitment could mean giving a set amount of money to your activity partner, or there might be something else that serves as a disincentive to giving up.

An Extra Tip: Consider sending a daily email or text message to your accountability partner after engaging in your habit. How's that for commitment?

It's essential to be as specific as possible about the arrangement is set. And whatever you do, make sure your accountability partner is set. And who understands the importance of your new habit and takes it as seriously as you do.

JOIN A SUPPORT GROUP

Support groups are yet another great tool. As I've said before, it is absolutely crucial that you surround yourself with people that will encourage you to achieve your goal. Being part of a group of people whose objectives are similar to yours will certainly help you tremendously. If your daily habit is part of a larger goal, joining a support group is one of the best things you can do. Can you think of a group you could join that would support your new habit? If not, the internet is a great place to start. There are forums dedicated to self-improvement and changing your habits. There are also meetups for people interested in forming new habits, as well as meetups for people that are already engaging in a specific habit (such as jogging, meditating, or running). You may not have many people in your life who are focused on self-improvement, but meeting others who are trying to build new habits is easier than you think!

BE WILLING TO INVEST IN YOURSELF

If you're genuinely committed to make changes in your life, you should be willing to put a little money towards it. If your habit is truly important, you'll probably be willing to put quite a bit of money towards it. Imagine if you had paid $200 for this book. How much more committed do you think you would be? It's highly likely that you would be determined to get the most out of it. No one wants to waste money, especially large sums of it.

As such, you can use money as an incentive to stick to your goals. If you've been consistently struggling to adopt a new habit, you can increase your level of commitment by investing in something to help you, whether it's a book, course, therapist, or coach. I've purchased some great resources over the years, and they've served as powerful incentives to push through obstacles and make the changes I desire.

More specifically, I tried many times to implement a daily morning ritual. I knew it would help me start my day on a good note and maintain a positive mindset. I wanted it to include things like setting my goals for the day, meditating, repeating positive affirmations, performing gratitude exercises. However, I failed miserably. And repeatedly. I finally wound up investing in a program to help me create and stick to my morning ritual. I spent $37, but I've maintained my new morning ritual for several months now and feel confident that I will continue to do so for years to come. The investment was more than worth it!

I'm a strong believer in investing in structured programs rather than wasting time trying to compile scattered information that may or may not give you results. It's often very time-consuming and exhausting, to say nothing of how difficult it is to verify the accuracy of what you find. As a result, I invest as much money in myself as I can, and I highly recommend you do the same.

Your 30-Day Challenge

What could be better than a 30-Day Challenge to strengthen your commitment to your new habit? My goal is to help you get through the challenge, and the workbook is one of multiple ways in which I will support you throughout this challenge. Consider me an accountability partner, if you will. Remember, you can have more than one!

At this point, you've gotten a lot of information about the dos and don'ts of creating new habits and sticking to them. Now it's time to start putting what you're learning into action. Are you ready to embark on the 30-Day Challenge? The fact that you're still reading tells me that you are!

If you want, you can send me an email at thibaut.meurisse@gmail.com with a simple "YES" or (better yet!) with a "YES" AND a description of what you're committing to. I'm more than happy to act as your accountability partner, and look forward to hearing from you very soon!

Execute Like A Champion

Just Get Started: The Power of Tiny Habits

Sometimes the habits you want to implement in your life seem so challenging that you don't know where to start. Remember, it's EXTREMELY important that you believe in your ability to consistently implement your new habit. This kind of belief can be a struggle for many of us, but starting small is a great way to work around it. If your new habit feels too overwhelming, try a smaller, modified version of it that feels manageable to you.

Tiny Habits are very powerful and have multiple benefits. Even the simplest habits are easy to neglect. By enabling you to lower the bar to a level that's more comfortable, Tiny Habits make it much easier to ensure you take consistent action. They also decrease the amount of willpower you have to use to implement the habit. Our brains don't like change and our minds love efficiency, minimizing the use of willpower is a wonderful thing.

Consistency Over Intensity

If there's only one thing you remember from this book it should be the fact that **consistency is far more important than intensity.**

If your habit requires so much energy that you can't sustain it long enough for it to become automatic and ingrained in your subconscious, you'll be very unlikely to succeed in implementing it. You run the risk of crashing and burning, and the harder the task is the more you are likely to procrastinate. This is yet another area where Tiny Habits come in handy.

Below are examples of Tiny Habits that you can incorporate into your life without exhausting yourself:

- **Name:** The Running Habit
- **How to Do It:** Just put your shoes on and go.

- **Name:** The Push-up Habit

- **How to Do It**: Do a push-up. And yes, I mean 'a' push-up. Just one.

- **Name:** The Writing Habit
- **What to Do:** Open whatever you use to create documents and start writing something. It can be anything you want, as long as you're writing.

- **Name:** The Diet Habit
- **What to Do:** Eat an apple. They say an apple a day keeps the doctor away (and what if they're right?)

- **Name:** Setting daily written goals
- **What to Do:** Write one simple goal and achieve it.

Is the habit you're currently trying to implement a challenging one? If so, how could you make it easier to get started? Think of a way to turn it into a smaller, more manageable habit.

I did this with meditation not too long ago. I really wanted to get back into it, but I knew that diving into it headfirst would probably be too intense. I made it easier by working it into my morning ritual and starting with just 3 minutes. It's been about 2 weeks and I'm already up to 9 minutes. See how daunting things can become totally doable just by scaling them down a bit?

You may be wondering whether you should scale things back and start smaller. That's a good question, and the answer will vary from person to person. That said, the following question will help you figure out what's right for you: Will you be able to perform your habit every day for the next 30 days even when you're tired or extremely busy? If the answer is yes, you're golden. If not, then you need to consider modifying your habit until you can say yes to that question.

NEVER SKIP TWICE

New habits are very easy to skip and you might think that it isn't a big deal. However, nothing could be farther from the truth. There are many people who say that skipping a new habit twice in a row has a devastating effect on your ability to stick with it. I've had more than one habit fade away after skipping it twice, and I've seen the same thing happen to other people on multiple occasions (New Year's resolutions, anyone?). Considering how hard it can be to make a new habit automatic, I would say the Two Skips Phenomenon is very real. Unless the habit is a well-established part of your subconscious, skipping it twice in a row comes with major risks, none of which are worth taking.

As harmless as two skips may seem, its dangers make a lot of sense if you really think about it. Skipping a fresh habit twice sends a signal to your brain that the habit isn't that important after all. If skipping it twice is okay, it must be pretty insignificant.

Remember, your brain doesn't like change. It's geared towards efficiency, which can make it lazy in a way. It likes to keep things automated and predictable. Disrupting this is hard enough, don't make it worse by sending it mixed signals about whether your habit is important. When that happens, your brain will ultimately view the habit as irrelevant and sabotage your efforts to work it into your life.

Want to know the best way to keep yourself from skipping a habit twice? Don't even skip it once!

PREPARE A CONTINGENCY PLAN

While it's best to never skip your habit, sometimes that's easier said than done. Nobody is perfect. We can't get around the fact that you very well may skip your habit at some point. What we can do, however, is anticipate this issue and combat it with a contingency plan. If you do wind up skipping a habit, the contingency plan will get you back on track. Let's say your habit is 15 minutes of meditation every morning. If you wake up late one morning and don't have time to meditate, you can decide to do it as soon as you come home from work.

You should always be honest with yourself and have a clear reason as to why you're skipping your habit. More importantly, you should identify likely obstacles and prepare an IF... THEN plan in advance.

I SUCK. SO WHAT?

As Tynan mentioned in his book *Superhuman by Habit*, it's better to do poorly at something than it is to just skip it. It's better to perform your tasks and push through fatigue than it is to skip it and rest. You might not do so well at them, but it's still much better than doing nothing.

Lack of consistency is one of the main reasons we end up quitting our new habits. There will be days were you really feel tired and don't feel like doing anything. There may be days when you want to procrastinate because you're afraid of failing. In these moments, it's best to get started anyway. Give yourself the permission to suck at what you're doing if that's what it takes for you to get it done. Just tell yourself that you'll give it a shot for a few minutes and see what happens. More often than not, the momentum gained by starting your task will allow you to accomplish more than you expect. If you're haunted by fears of doing a bad job, just take a deep breath and say, "I suck. So what?" Then carry on and tackle that task, knowing that whatever you do is a step forward, regardless of how well you do it.

DON'T BLAME YOURSELF

Sometimes it's tempting to blame yourself for skipping your habit, but that won't help you succeed at implementing it. In fact, it's one of the many tricks your mind will use to make you give up on your new habit. Your brain is lazy and will be more than happy to give up that new habit and go back to "normal". Don't fall for that! Remember, consistency is key. If you happen to skip a habit once, make sure you don't skip it the next day. Do it poorly if you need to. But whatever you do, don't lose your momentum. If you can manage that, you'll be just fine.

To help you here is a quote on self-compassion from the book *The Willpower Instinct* by Kelly McGonigal. I found it to be quite true.

"When we do experience setbacks – which we will – we need to forgive those failures, and not use them as an excuse to give in or give up. When it comes to increasing self-control, self-compassion is a far better strategy than beating ourselves up."-Kelly McGonigal

ACTIONS VS. RESULTS: WHAT REALLY MATTERS?

Have you ever felt that you weren't good enough? If so, you're definitely not alone. Almost everyone feels or has felt that way at some point. This is actually one of the main reasons we procrastinate and fail to take consistent action. We're afraid of being inept and unable to do a good job. If your new habit is challenging, you may be afraid that you won't perform as well as you'd like to. This is especially true if you're a perfectionist.

Unfortunately, most societies and school systems condition us to be result-oriented rather than process-oriented. As children, we are praised for our accomplishments, whether it's learning to walk, getting good grades, or winning a sports game.

This may not seem particularly harmful, but there's actually a major problem with it. This approach teaches us that it's the end result that counts, not the actions that led to it.

In reality, the reverse is true. The process matters much more than the result. Our brain is such an incredible machine that, if you keep taking the right actions, it will eventually figure things out. Your brain will learn through "failures" and a process of trial-and-error until you finally get the results you want. If you can keep trying until you get what you want and take each so-called failure as a learning experience, you'll be building more strength and confidence than you ever imagined. After all, being conditioned to focus on results is the reason we're so afraid of failing.

For clarity's sake, let's take a look at a real-life example of what I'm talking about. Let's say you're a blogger and you've decided to write 500 words each day. If you're writing just to write, 500 words isn't much, but you're probably writing with a specific objective in mind.

Maybe you're in the process of writing a book. Or perhaps you have a great idea for a blog post and want to produce high-quality work that will have a real impact on your readers.

It's easy to imagine why you'd be tempted to procrastinate in this situation. You might worry that what you write won't be good enough for your readers, or that your book will get rejected by publishers. These fears may be crippling enough to stop you in your tracks.

You don't have to be ruled by fear, however. You can overcome it by shifting your focus. Instead of worrying about the end result of your labors (writing great content or getting published), focus on taking the right action. In this case, the right action is pretty simple: Just sit at your desk and start typing until you reach 500 words.

Taking the right action means doing what you know is right regardless of the outcome. You know that you want to write 500 words every day. That is your right action. What sounds worse: writing something that's less than your best, or doing nothing because you're scared, tired, or uninspired? Are you going to wait until you think you can write something phenomenal, or are you just going to get started anyway?

You'll come to find that you're better off doing something than nothing, even if what you do doesn't turn out that well. We learn by doing, not by procrastinating.

Extra Tip: Erase the traditional definition of failure from your mind. What many people see as failure is actually feedback. It's a learning opportunity, an unavoidable stepping stone on the path to mastery and success. Failure goes hand in hand with success. Make no mistake however, failure is real. Fortunately, there are only two things that can lead you to true failure: Never trying or failing to learn from your mistakes. The good news is that these things are choices, and it's completely within your power not to avoid them.

The Power of the Right Action Framework

If you understand it well and practice it regularly, The Right Action Framework (the method of focusing on actions rather than results) is an extremely powerful tool. It allows you to take action while decreasing your anxiety about the results. The Right Action Framework redefines the notion of failure, but it also redefines the notion of success. This framework defines success as taking the right action, NOT as getting results. Getting results without taking the right action doesn't qualify as success. If you succeed via luck, doing something that goes against your right action, or engaging unethical behavior, your success would be invalidated by your flawed process.

In a nutshell, true failure means not taking action, taking the wrong action, or neglecting to learn from your mistakes.

Tips: Take a moment to reward yourself each time you take the right action. That will train your mind to focus on the process of taking action rather than on the results.

Procrastination? What's that?

Okay, you're now armed with several tools. Let's take a look at them:

- Having a strong why (Should vs. Want)
- Starting super small (Tiny Habits)
- Accepting a flawed performance (I suck so what?)
- Avoiding self-blame
- Taking the right action

So what excuses do you have left to procrastinate or skip your habits? Not many, right?

THE 21-DAY MYTH

How much time do you really need until your new habits are fully transferred to your subconscious mind? You may be familiar with the famous "It takes 21 days to form a new habit" theory, but I think that's mostly BS. Believing in it can be very counterproductive. In reality, everybody is different, and the amount of time it takes for a habit to become automatic varies from person to person.

According to a 2009 study on habits published in the *European Journal of Social Psychology*, it took an average of 66 days for participants to fully adopt a new habit. But, of course, this is an average based on the varying results of multiple people. So how much time will it take you to form your new habits?

The answer is: Nobody knows. It could take 3 weeks or several months, but it doesn't matter in the end. A habit is, by definition, something you want to do every day for years to come, so there's no need to worry about how long it will take to fully assimilate it. You have plenty of time!

If you hold yourself to the 21-day rule, you'll probably get pretty discouraged if you're still struggling after three weeks. You might feel like you're abnormal and ultimately quit your habit. **Forget about the 21 days. Consider the fact that it may take longer than that, and stay consistent with your habits each and every day.**

How fast you form a new habit depends on the following 4 factors:

1. Your specific situation.
2. How challenging the new habit is.
3. The strength of your "why".
4. Your level of motivation.

IDENTIFY YOUR HIGH-LEVERAGE HABITS

Changing just one habit in your life can create great results long-term, particularly because new habits have a strong effect on current habits. If you change your habits strategically, you can maximize the amount of positive change you experience.

Think of it this way: If you make going to bed early a habit, you may find yourself meditating, exercising, or working on your side business in the morning. The increased energy that comes from getting more rest will positively impact your productivity, mood, and ability to follow through with preexistent habits. This holds true for any new habit; it tends to make it easier to stick to the ones you already have.

Now take a look at your current habits. Are there any pivotal habits around which many others are revolving? What is the one habit that, if implemented, would have the most positive impact on your life?

SETTING UP TRIGGERS

You may be wondering about when and how to schedule your habits. Since consistency is the cornerstone of developing your new habit, you want to schedule it in a   way that minimizes your risk of skipping it. The best way to do that is to set up a trigger for that specific habit. By anchoring your habit around a specific daily event, you make it easier to create an automatic pattern and ensure consistency.

There are a variety of potential triggers you can use. For instance, you could choose to engage in your habit after your shower or as soon as you wake up.

Choose a Rock-solid Trigger

The most effective triggers are things that you do every day at the same time, such as having breakfast, brushing your teeth, or walking your pet. If your trigger is weak, you're already shooting yourself in the foot. If the trigger is eating breakfast, but you don't always have a morning meal, you're going to have trouble staying on track with your habit.

Act AFTER Your Trigger

It's better to perform your new habit after the trigger and not before it. This makes it easier for you to remember. Let's say you've chosen showering as a trigger for meditation. If you try to meditate before your showers you'll tend to think, "Oh, I almost forgot, it's meditation time" (which we all know can easily lead to just plain forgetting meditation time). If you do it after your showers however, you'll think something along the lines of "I'm done with my shower, so now it's meditation time."

Make a List of Triggers

Make a list of the tasks you do 7 days a week. This list shouldn't be very long. Now ask yourself: What would be the best trigger for my habit?

Let's say you want to meditate every day. Going back to the meditation example, is it better to do it as soon as you wake up? Would you prefer to do it after you take a shower? Or maybe you'd rather do it after breakfast? Choosing the trigger gives you the best possible chance of sticking to your habit.

CREATING SERIES OF HABITS

Once you've successfully implemented your first habit, you can go bigger and create a series of habits. A chain of habits is just multiple habits that occur one after the other. You complete one, and then start the next. By repeating this process you can create powerful series of habits that will help you make positive changes in your life. This offers many benefits, and creates clear patterns that will become automatic over time.

Let's say I've been meditating consistently for the past 2 months and want to start writing my goals down on a daily basis. I would simply add that habit into my life with my meditation practice as its trigger and voila: I'd have a budding series of habits. I'd add a third habit once the second one became solid, and keep going from there. I would eventually have a strong chain to lean on.

A Potential Pitfall

If used effectively, a series of habits is very powerful. That said, it's absolutely crucial to ensure that your current habit is strong enough to support the addition of another one. If you have a series of 5 habits, but most of them are pretty new, you could end up skipping one or two and ultimately destroy them all.

Series of Habits Example

A morning ritual is an excellent example of a typical series of habits. A morning ritual is simply a succession of habits that ensure you start your morning in a positive way that sets you up for a successful day. Most successful people have some kind of morning ritual.

Here is a list of activities that might be included in a morning ritual:

- Meditating.
- Walking/running/stretching, etc.
- Setting daily goals.
- Doing gratitude exercises.
- Reciting positive affirmations.
- Reading books.
- Watching motivational videos.
- Eating a healthy breakfast.

Do you have a morning ritual? If not, I highly recommend creating one. It's one of the most effective ways to ensure you stay consistent with your habits. It also allows you to leverage your series of habits. If you commit to sticking with your morning ritual, you'll be able to maintain your habits for as long as you want.

Morning rituals are adaptable, so you can tweak yours when necessary to increase its effectiveness and tailor it to your needs. If reciting affirmations is part of your morning ritual, for instance, you can modify the affirmations as your goals evolve.

Example: As I write this book, I could design my morning ritual around my goal of completing it. Affirmations should remind you of what excites you about what you're doing. In this example, my affirmations would be linked to my current goal, and would include the following statements, or something similar:

- I'm excited about writing an incredible book that will impact the lives of thousands of people around the world.
- I'm excited about creating great books that will inspire thousands of people to set goals, find their passion, and attain the career of their dreams.

- I'm excited about writing content that will enable thousands of people to positively impact those around them and society as a whole.

The affirmations you use are totally up to you. As you go through the process you'll find affirmations that will resonate with you and strengthen your "why". What does and doesn't resonate can change over time, but your morning rituals are wonderfully malleable.

If you ever struggle to find affirmations that speak to you, ask yourself why you're doing what you're doing. In this case, I would ask myself why I'm writing this book and what makes it so important? Ask these questions until you find answers that inspire you.

Later on, you might want to change your affirmations if you decide to shift your focus to a different area of your life. Going back to our example, I might decide to concentrate on eliminating harmful beliefs and realize that I hold limiting beliefs regarding money* that are preventing me from reaching my ideal income. I could then use my morning ritual as a way to overcome these limiting beliefs. I could recite affirmations on wealth or read books about building wealth to help me shift my mindset. Or I could do some money-related exercises to dig deep and get to the root of the negative belief.

*See the article *4 Disempowering Beliefs About Money That Keep You Poor* for more information about how your beliefs affect your finances.

Interestingly enough, creating my morning ritual wasn't easy. Writing books on habits and goal-setting doesn't mean that I have a magical superpower that enables me to effortlessly form new habits, but I wish it did! As I mentioned in the section on investing money, I failed many times in my attempt to create a morning ritual. I had watched videos about it, I understood the concept, and I even knew what kind of habits I could incorporate into it. Yet I continued to fail until I purchased a program to help me stick to it.

What about you? What series of habits would you like to create in the future? What would your ideal morning ritual look like?

Examples of Morning Rituals

As we discussed earlier, most successful people have some kind of morning rituals. Why? Because it is very difficult to be successful if you don't set yourself up for it on a daily basis. Some people start their day eating unhealthy food and watching the news, passively absorbing negativity and slowly diminishing their health. But successful people are proactive. They decide how they want to feel and what they want to accomplish throughout the day. They set their goals for the day, practice gratitude, and ask themselves powerful questions.

For instance, Benjamin Franklin would start every morning with a seemingly simple question: "What good shall I do this day?" Brian Tracy reads inspirational books for 30 to 60 minutes each morning before setting his goals. How about you? Are you reactive or are you proactive? Do you choose how you want to feel every morning, or do you simply react to your environment? Are you the type of person who hits the snooze button several times, rushes to get ready, grabs a coffee on the way to work and hopes for the best? Or are you the type of person who meditates, exercises, and sets clear goals for the day?

Let's take a look at the morning rituals of some very successful people.
Tony Robbins

Tony Robbins is quite possibly the most famous coach and motivational speaker in the world. Here's what his morning ritual looks like:

1. Jump into a cold pool or use whole body cryotherapy.
2. Do some breathing exercises.
3. Express gratitude. He picks 3 things he's grateful for, making sure his list includes one very small thing like the wind on his face.
4. Pray for strength and wish good things for his family, friends, and clients.

Kenneth Chenault, CEO of American Express

Chenault's ritual centers around goal-setting. Before leaving the office, the last thing he does is to write down the top three things he wants to accomplish the next day. He then uses this list to start the following day.

Steve Jobs

His morning ritual centered around asking powerful questions. He detailed it in the following quote:

"For the past 33 years, I have looked in the mirror every morning and asked myself: 'If today were the last day of my life, would I want to do what I am about to do today?'

And whenever the answer has been 'No' for too many days in a row, I know I need to change something."

THE 7 MOST POWERFUL (YET SIMPLE) HABITS TO HAVE IN LIFE

In this section, I'd like to provide you with what I believe are some of the most powerful habits that you can have. These habits will have a profound impact in your life in the long run. This short list is far from being exhaustive, but it will give you some ideas for future habits you might want to incorporate into your daily life.

#1 SETTING DAILY GOALS.

Setting your goals every single day will, from my own experience, double (if not triple!) your productivity. To set your goals, just take a pen and a piece of paper (avoid typing on the computer) and make a list of 3 to 5 tasks you want to accomplish for the day. Then, prioritize your tasks by numbering them in order of importance. Start working on your first task until you complete it and move to the next one. Repeat the process. If you can do this on a daily basis you're bound to get a lot done. To learn more about this process, feel free to refer to my goal-setting book.

#2 READING YOUR GOALS EVERY DAY.

This is a powerful way to ensure that you stay on track with your goals. Ideally, you should think of your goals as often as possible. When things get busy, it's very easy to forget about our goals, but reading them out loud on a daily basis can prevent that from happening. You shouldn't just read your goals, however, you should also ask yourself why they're so important. There has to be a strong reason behind your goals if you're going to successfully work on them. If, for instance, my goal is to earn $600 a month from my books, I'd need to state this in a way that reminds me of why this goal matters to me. I would say, "By December 31st 2016, I'll be earning $600 per month from Kindle Publishing and impacting the lives of thousands of people around the world." I could also say "By December 31st 2016, I'll be earning $600 per month from Kindle Publishing and inspiring thousands of people to set goals, change their habits, and become role models for those around them." It's equally important to take a moment to visualize your goals and how achieving them would feel.

#3 MEDITATING

Meditation provides a plethora of benefits. I won't go through them all, but you can check out this http://liveanddare.com/benefits-of-meditation/ if you want to learn more about them. It mentions over 76 scientific benefits!

You can begin with just a few minutes a day. There are many ways to meditate, but it can be as simple as closing your eyes and focusing on your breath. There are also several good books for beginners that can help you get started.

#4 PRACTICING GRATITUDE.

Forgetting to express gratitude is a major cause of unhappiness for many of us. We take everything for granted and don't fully appreciate the little things in life (or even the big ones). There's a hilarious comedy sketch from Louis CK about airplanes and the way people take technology for granted that illustrates this perfectly. Check it out below.

"'It was the worst day of my life. First of all, we didn't board for twenty minutes, and then we get on the plane and they made us sit there on the runway...' Oh really, what happened next? Did you fly through the air incredibly, like a bird? Did you partake in the miracle of human flight you non-contributing zero?! You're flying! It's amazing! Everybody on every plane should just constantly be going: 'Oh my God! Wow!' You're flying! You're sitting in a chair, in the sky!" – Louis CK

Every day during my morning ritual, I ask myself what I'm grateful for. I then spend a few minutes thinking about everything that crosses my mind. You don't have to come up with anything major, it's okay to think about the little things. The following list will make it easier to practice gratitude by reminding you of some basic things you can be grateful for:

- Amazon, YouTube, and other such platforms that provide access to an endless supply of knowledge at little to no cost.
- Living in one of history's most exciting time periods. Kids will study our time period a thousand years from now and be amazed at the rapid increases in technology. We've gone from telegrams and carriages to race cars, camera phones, internet access, and virtual reality (among other amazing things) in less than 150 years. It's incredible!
- Having food, shelter, running water, and electricity.
- Having a phone that enables you to communicate with your friends and family no matter how far apart you are.

The list is endless!

I say what I'm grateful for out loud, but some people prefer creating a written gratitude list. The trick is to feel genuine gratitude as you contemplate the things on your list. As Jim Rohn says, "Our emotions need to be as educated as our intellect." So be patient and stick with this habit. I can guarantee it will pay off in the long-run.

#5 CONSUMING MOTIVATIONAL BOOKS AND VIDEOS.

In the words of Zig Ziglar, "People often say that motivation doesn't last. Well, neither does bathing – that's why we recommend it daily." No matter how exciting your goals may be, there will be time when you won't feel like doing anything.

Feeding your mind with inspirational material on a daily basis will help you stay motivated for the long-haul. If you can't find the time to read, you can also listen to uplifting audiobooks. In fact, I have a Jim Rohn audiobook that I've listened to over 100 times.

#6 SELF-REFLECTING.

Taking a few minutes to reflect upon your day is a very effective way to improve yourself. Self-reflection is one of the best ways to supercharge your growth. When you analyze the events of your day, consider asking yourself the following questions:

- What did I do well today?
- What could I have done better?
- What can I learn from today?
- What will I do differently in the future?

#7 EXERCISING DAILY.

You already know that you should get some exercise each day, so I'm not going to try to convince you. These days, most of us spend too much time sitting down and looking at our televisions or computers.

According to Dr. James Levine, author of *Get Up! Why your Chair is Killing You and What You Can Do About It*, every hour that you spend sitting cuts off 3 hours of your life. I haven't read this book yet, but I plan to check it out soon.

I might even invest in a treadmill desk or at least a standing desk. Did you know that some desks allow you to switch between standing and sitting with just one touch? Sounds pretty cool! So, what kind of exercise are you going to do each day?

TAKE ACTION RIGHT NOW OR ELSE...

I have one question for you: Have you started to take action and implement a new, powerful habit in your life? If not, will you?

Will you be the person who sets goals, finds their passion, creates a fulfilling career, and becomes an inspiration to those around them? It would be a great honor for me to have helped you form positive, life-changing habits in some way, and I would love to hear from you regarding your progress.

After releasing my book on goal setting, I received comments from people who told me that it made a real impact on their lives. These people put the book's contents to use and turned the knowledge they received into tangible result. To my delight, one of my readers took immediate action upon reading my book.

"I myself have a lofty goal that I have only just begun to work on, and after reading this book I stopped everything and used the steps to lay out a plan for not only how I am going to accomplish this, but when." – Mark Richmond, US

Another reader began to immediately impact others by sharing the book with her kids.

"Your book has been an inspiration in my life and I want to thank you. I'm halfway through your book and I want to give to my kids as well. – Kelly D.

It goes without saying that I would love to hear more stories like that from my readers.

On the other hand, a colleague who knew of my book asked to have a look at it after spotting a Kindle in my bag. I said yes and, as she looked over it, I suggested she buy it because it was on sale for just $1 at the time. $1 doesn't seem likely to break the bank, does it?   Even so, she said, "I'll think about it" in a very serious tone. For those who don't know, "I'll think about it" almost always means NO in Japan.

So who do you want to be, the person who invests in themselves and gets results, or the person who doesn't value themselves enough to invest in resources that will help them reach their goals?

YOUR HABIT FORMATION CHECKLIST

We covered a lot in this book, and I would like to briefly summarize the steps you need to follow when implementing a new habit in your life. You can use this summary as a checklist for your new habit.

PREPARE YOURSELF AND YOUR ENVIRONMENT

- **Select a high-impact habit** that will produce the greatest results in your life.
- **Make a list of all obstacles** that could make you give up on that habit.
- **Design a supportive environment** for your habit (make it as easy as possible by removing or minimizing your obstacles).

STRENGTHEN YOUR COMMITMENT

- Make a real commitment to yourself- Give it 100%.
- **Make sure you have a strong "why"**- Is it something you **want** or something you believe you **should** do?
- **Find an accountability partner or group**- It makes it easier to stay committed.
- **Invest your money**- Be willing to invest in books, programs, courses, or a coach if necessary.
- **Write down your habit** and why it is important to you.
- Undertake the 30-Day-Challenge.

EXECUTE

- **Select a trigger for your habit**- The trigger should be something you do every day. Make your habit easier to remember by engaging in it after the trigger, not before.
- **Start as small as you have to-** Make your habit easy to do, and assess how confident you are of your ability to stick to the habit during the next 30 days and beyond.
- **Focus on taking the right action**- Don't concentrate on results, just take the action you know is right without worrying about the results.

- **Don't blame yourself**- That's a trick of the mind designed to make you give up.
- **Don't skip your habit-** Do it poorly if you must, but always do it. Remember that skipping a habit more than once will destroy it.
- **Have an If... Then plan**- If you have no choice but to skip your habit, be aware of the reason for it and come up with an alternative (such as doing it later in the day).
- **Forget about the 21-Day myth**- Stay focused on your habit for as long as it takes to make it stick. After all, you want to be able to maintain it for years to come.

Once your habit is firmly established, work on a new one to begin the creation of a series of habits. And last but not least: always choose consistency over intensity.

Conclusion

I would like to congratulate you for staying with me until the end of this book. At this point, it's clear that your commitment is real. Now, the ball is in your court. Don't hesitate to go through this book when you need help. You may need to go over it several times as you attempt to create new habits. That's okay! If you have any question or feedback, please feel free to contact me at thibaut.meurisse@gmail.com.

What Do You Think?

I want to hear from you! Your thoughts and comments are important to me. If you enjoyed this book or found it useful **I'd be very grateful if you'd post a short review on Amazon**. Your support really does make a difference. I read all the reviews personally so I can get your feedback and make this book even better.

Thanks again for your support!

Final Words

Habits are the foundation of your success. I hope you'll use the information in this book to help you create powerful new habits in your life. Creating new habits or getting rid of existing ones is never easy. In fact, I can almost guarantee that you will fail several times in the process. When this happens, it is my hope that you will refer to this book, reread everything that applies to your situation, and try again. Habits aren't always hard to do, but they're very easy *not* to do.

About The Author

THIBAUT MEURISSE Thibaut Meurisse is a personal development blogger, author, and founder of whatispersonaldevelopment.org.

He has been featured on major personal development websites such as Lifehack, TinyBuddha, PickTheBrain, Stevenaitchison, Guidedmind, Dumblittleman or Finerminds.

Obsessed with self-improvement and fascinated by the power of the brain, his personal mission is to help people realize their full potential and reach higher levels of fulfillment and consciousness.

In love with foreign languages, he is French, writes in English, and has been living in Japan for the past 7 years.

You can connect with him on his facebook page https://www.facebook.com/whatispersonaldevelopment.org

Learn more about Thibaut at amazon.com/author/thibautmeurisse

Bibliography

Books

Goal Setting: The Ultimate Guide To Achieving Goals That Truly Excite You, Thibaut Meurisse

Habits Stacking: 97 Small Life Changes That Take Five Minutes or Less, S.J. Scott

Superhuman By Habit – A Guide to Becoming the Best Possible Version of Yourself, One Tiny Habit at a time, Tynan

The Willpower Instinct, Kelly McGonigal

Videos

The Power of Routines – How your Daily Routine Holds you Back From Your Dreams Actualized.org (24mn)

Bad Habits – A Live Exercise for Dropping Any Habit For Good, Actualized.org (24mn)

Website

James Clear website

Goal Setting: The Ultimate Guide To Achieving Goals That Truly Excite You – Include a Step-By-Step Workbook

PREVIEW

Introduction

"Mr. Rohn, let me see your current list of goals. I've had a lot of experience and I've been out here for a while, so let's go over them and maybe I can really give you some good ideas." And I said, "I don't have a list." He said, " Well, if you don't have a list of your goals, I can guess your bank balance within a few hundred dollars." And he did. – Jim Rohn, The Jim Rohn Guide to Goal Setting

I would like to thank you for downloading this e-book. In doing so, you have already shown your commitment to bettering your life by setting goals that truly excite you. You have joined those who have made the decision to take more control over their lives and give less power to circumstances. It's important to think about what where you want to be, whether it's one month, six months, one year, five years or even a decade or more from now. Taking the time to identify the goals you wish to accomplish is the best way to make sure that you're going into the right direction. It will also keep you from pursuing goals that won't fulfill you.

Deciding to set goals is probably one of the most important decisions you can make, but most people don't set clear goals in their life. It's almost as if they believe they have no control over their life. As such, they wander through life heavily influenced by the circumstances and people around them. They give their power away to their environments instead of using it to create the lives they desire. They achieve far les than they would if they took the time to plan their lives and set specific goals.

Keep in mind, however, that having goals in and of itself is not enough. In fact, having goals that are unclear or out of alignment with what you want can be almost as bad as having none at all. Unfortunately, many goal setters spend years in dogged pursuit of a particular goal only to achieve it and realize that isn't what they genuinely wanted. This e-book will help you avoid that. Setting specific goals is one of the best decisions I've made in my life and the information within this book will give you an opportunity to do the same.

I first created a list of goals back in September of 2014 while in the process of building my website. Looking back, I often wonder why I'd never done it before and why I never learned about it in school. Setting goals is par for the course when it comes to personal development, however.

I believe that we all have the potential to accomplish great things in life. However, many of us never learned to tap into our intrinsic ability to self-motivate. We spend our childhoods studying to get good grades and trying to fit in in an attempt to please our parents, teachers, and peers. We then spend our adulthoods working for money and other external motivators. Our tendency to rely upon outside motivators is ironic considering how ineffective they are. Studies show that extrinsic motivators such as money are less efficient than intrinsic motivators like autonomy, self-mastery, or finding purpose. The carrot and stick approach is still in frequent use these days, but it's far from ideal. The reality is that intrinsic motivation yields better results and provides a greater sense of fulfillment than extrinsic motivation does.

Fortunately, learning to set the right goals will help you tap into your intrinsic motivation and allow you to uncover your hidden potential. This book is intended to help you figure out what you want to achieve and the kind of life you wish to create for yourself. I want you to set goals that inspire you, stir your soul, and make you want to jump out of bed every morning. Goal setting might seem intimidating, but it's more than worth it!

What you will learn in this book:

Within this book, you'll find a comprehensive method to achieve your goals. You won't just learn how to set goals effectively, you'll also learn to think better thoughts, overcome obstacles, and persevere until you reach your goal.

This Book Will:

1) Give you the opportunity to discover and set goals that genuinely matter to you
2) Help you set short-term, mid-term, and long-term goals in multiple areas of your life.
3) Help you realize your potential and achieve more than you thought possible.
4) Provide you with an effective strategy to achieve the goals you set.
5) Enable you to avoid the obstacles you will encounter while working towards your goals.

This book is full of valuable information, but remember that how much you get out of it is largely dependent upon how committed you are to implementing it. The ball is in your court!

Why goal Setting is important

People without goals are doomed to work forever for people who do have goals – Brian Tracy

Setting goals gives direction to your subconscious mind

Your automatic creative mechanism is teleological. That is, it operates in terms of goals and end results. Once you give it a definite goal to achieve, you can depend upon its automatic guidance system to take you to that goal much better than "you" ever could by conscious thought. "You" supply the goal by thinking in terms of end results. Your automatic mechanism them supplies the means whereby. – Maxwell Maltz

Did you know your subconscious mind could help you achieve your goal? Setting goals gives you a direction in life, but vague goals like making more money or being happy won't lead to a fulfilling life. Your subconscious mind is like a powerful machine, and understanding how it works is a big part of successful goal setting. Hypnotherapist Joseph Clough compares it to a GPS whereas Maxwell Maltz, author of Psycho-Cybernetics, calls it a mechanical goal-seeking device. If you put an address into your GPS, it will do whatever it can to reach your destination. The subconscious mind behaves similarly. Have you ever learned a new word only to find yourself hearing it everywhere you go? That's an example of your brain "priming". In other words, it's scanning your environment for all information relevant to the word, phrase, or details you've given it. As such, setting clear goals gives you a greater chance of accomplishing them. It sends a strong signal to your subconscious mind, which allows it to unleash its focusing power and look for any opportunities to achieve the goal. We talk more about the importance of specific goals later.

Setting goals empowers you

If you don't design your own life plan, chances are you'll fall into someone else's plan. And guess what they have planned for you? Not much. – Jim Rohn

Are you the one choosing your goals? Or are others choosing them for you? When you start setting intentions, you stop giving away your power.

When you start setting objectives in all the main areas of your life such as finances, relationships, career, and health, you stop giving power away and start empowering yourself. You make a conscious choice to become the creator of your life and begin to take responsibility in every aspect of your life.

Imagine the difference it would make in your life if you were to take the time to figure out your goals for the future. If you knew how much you wanted to earn in 5 years, how long you wanted to live, and where you'd like to be in 20 years, what would you do differently?

Setting goals increases self-esteem

High self-esteem seeks the challenge and stimulation of worthwhile and demanding goals. Reaching such goals nurtures good self-esteem. Low self-esteem seeks the safety of the familiar and undemanding. Confining oneself to the familiar and undemanding serves to weaken self-esteem. – Nathaniel Branden

Did you know that you could increase your self-esteem by setting clear goals? It's worth mentioning that having clear goals and achieving them builds and reinforces our self-esteem. In fact, Nathaniel Branden (author of *The Six Pillars Of Self-Esteem*) states that part of our self-esteem comes from a "disposition to experience ourselves as competent to cope with life's challenges". With every achievement we accomplish, we feel better equipped to deal with other goals and life challenges. In *The Pursuit of Happiness* David G. Myers shows that high self-esteem is one of the best predictors of personal happiness. Consistently accomplishing the goals you set is one of the most efficient ways to build self-esteem.

Goal setting changes your reality

The value of goals is not in the future they describe, but the change in perception of reality they foster – David Allen, Getting Things Done

Setting goals is a valuable process on its own, regardless of whether or not you'll achieve them. You're probably wondering why that's the case. Well, there are several reasons. Goal setting helps you think about your future, gives you an opportunity to reflect on your values, and helps you discover what matters most. It will bring clarity and allow you to see the bigger picture of your life. It doesn't get much more valuable than that.

Setting goals will also allow you to reconstruct your reality and realize that dreams you previously thought unattainable are in fact achievable. It all starts with identifying your real desires, no matter how ambitious they are. In so doing, you'll begin the process of overcoming your limiting beliefs. Limiting beliefs stem from past experiences and make it harder to get the life you want. You'll soon realize how restrictive limiting beliefs are and just how many of them stem from repetitive messages received from family, friends, and the media.

Lastly, goal setting will give you the opportunity to assess your current situation and close the gap between where you are and where you want to be.

Setting goals is good for your health

Use goals to live longer. No medicine in the world – and your physician will bear this out – is as powerful in bringing about life as is the desire to do something. – David J. Schwartz, The Magic Of Thinking Big

Dan Buettner, the author of *The Blue Zone: Lessons for Living Longer From the People Who've Lived The Longest*, identified 10 characteristics shared by those who live to 100. He identified "having a life purpose" as one of them. Setting goals that fully excite you is one of the best medicines and will work wonders for your health. An alarming number of people die within a few years of retirement. I believe this is partly because they no longer have exciting goals to motivate them, something that is especially likely for those who heavily identified with their job. What about you? Have you found goals that will motivate you well into old age?

How to set goals

The key to goal setting is for you to think on paper. Successful men and women think with a pen in their hands; unsuccessful people do not. –
Brian Tracy

You can learn more at **amazon.com/author/thibautmeurisse**

43336620R00040

Made in the USA
Middletown, DE
22 April 2019